Namasté

A spiritual romance, a self-help adventure, and a new way of being

By Declan Kerr

Namasté is published by aaah publications
October 2007

465 Buxton Road, Great Moor, Stockport. SK2 7HE

The aaah publications website address is
"http://www.aaahpublications.com" www.aaahpublications.com

A catalogue record of this book is available from the British Library

ISBN 978-0-9556040-2-7

Design and print is by Stonebrook print & design of Wallsend, Newcastle-upon-Tyne
www.stonebrook.co.uk

Dedication

This book is dedicated to my gorgeous wife Angela Kerr

Acknowledgments

To Diana Cooper who is truly inspirational and from whom I have learned and continue to learn so much

Vernon Frost for his insights and the triangle of eternal truth

Harry Owen and Omar Rafiqi for the best discussions

My fabulous friends who meet each Monday at the Angel Healing Centre in Stockport who have road-tested the grail energy which is described here

Peter and the team at Stonebrook print & design who have brought this script to life and Lee Phillips at Stonebrook in particular

And Angela Kerr who has supported me throughout trusting that I was following my star

Thankyou all

Declan

Contents

Introduction

Namasté is a spiritual romance, a self-help adventure, and introduces new energies and a new way of being in those energies.

The word namasté is a spiritual greeting:

"I honour the spirit in you" is where this started. As the book has developed Namasté has gained additional meaning. It is clear that the spirit in you is the spirit in me. Separate and one. And once the romance and the adventure are added in it is clear that this light is significant.

The romance is falling in love with life. All of the delights of life plus a new energy and new light in which we can experience it all over again in new and wonderful ways.

Self-help adventure is the search for the holy grail and experiencing grail energies. Not riding around on trusty steeds in exotic locations and prevailing over adversity or dastardly foes. More a case of, wouldn't you know, it was here all the time we just couldn't see it.

The grail energy confirms that the spirit in you and the spirit in me is brilliant, and brings an energy and a light which we haven't seen or experienced for a long time.

The grail energy also means uncovering dimension where there is room to live and breathe and create the life you wish for. Finding balance in duality, balance in paradox, and new doors.

This could also usher in heaven on earth. If that is what you choose. It's your life.

For my part I wish you a beautiful journey and hope you enjoy some of the light and energy in this book.

Namasté!

Declan

Part One: Romance with Life

Namasté

Namasté is a spiritual greeting. 'I salute the spirit in you'. It can also be used as an extension of this to mean 'the spirit in me says hello to the spirit in you' or 'the light in me says hello to the light in you'.

Another variation comes from the metaphysical teacher Vernon Frost who says "I honour the light and life within you"

In this book by saying Namasté I'm also saying, I wish you to be yourself. You have space here to be yourself.

This book was written expressly to encourage you to see yourself. How wonderful you are.

So Namasté: I salute the spirit in you, I honour the light and life within you and I ask you to be your own wonderful self.

Being ourselves can sometimes be a challenge. We may have spent a lot of time in our lives trying to please others, to get our needs met, to avoid painful situations, to get or keep a job, to get or keep a relationship and many other variations where we loose sight of ourself.

In any of these scenarios we may need to review or re-learn who we are and how to honour ourself.

If none of the above apply to you then bless you, you are a role model and more power to your elbow.

If some of the above has a familiar feel you may enjoy this sequence from Marianne Williamson's book "A Return to

Love". The lines are sometimes attributed to Nelson Mandela who quoted from it in his inaugural speech as President of South Africa in 1994.

Our Deepest Fear

"Our deepest fear is not that we are inadequate……

Our deepest fear is that we are powerful beyond measure.

It is our light, not our darkness that frightens us.

We ask ourselves, who am I to be brilliant, gorgeous, talented and fabulous?

Actually, who are you not to be ?

You are a child of God.

Your playing small doesn't serve the world.

There's nothing enlightened about shrinking so that other people won't feel insecure around you.

We were born to manifest the glory of God within us.

It's not just in some of us, it's in everyone.

And as we let our light shine we unconsciously give other people permission to do the same.

As we are liberated from our own fear our presence automatically liberates others "

Look Inside

I'm reminded as I write of a phrase Mahatma Ghandi used for his autobiography….'I have nothing new to teach the world. Truth and non-violence are as old as the hills' [2]

The truth as I understand it is inside me, and it is inside you. If this book is doing anything, it is intended to help remind you of your truth.

How do you take a look inside?

It will be in the way that is right for you. I'll suggest some things here and you'll experiment with them if it feels right. In this chapter and also some of the chapters which follow. If it doesn't feel right don't do it.

Start with re-acquainting yourself with your intuition.

It's located in your solar plexus. This is also where we feel or store-up a lot of emotion. It's your 'gut feeling'. It makes you feel sick when things are not right, or when your body needs a rest, or when you need to get some space away from a situation, a person or a place.

It's also a place of incredible joy when things are working well for you. You're 'in the flow', 'in your element', 'out of your mind'.

Find a quiet space and time. You'll need about 10 minutes. Switch-off any phones, and find somewhere comfortable to sit or lie down. Close your eyes.

---

2 "An Autobiography "M.K. Gandhi. Penguin classics 2001

Form your intention to get in touch with your intuition. You'd like to re-establish contact. Turn it into a game and play hide and seek.

Announce to your intuition that you're going to find it. It has to hide and you are counting to 10. When you've counted to ten announce you're coming ready or not. And start looking.

It will be hiding in a landscape, or amongst feelings, or within colours, or wherever your game takes you. You are interested to know what it looks like and what it feels like.

Simply be open to what you are seeing or feeling. Give the game a chance, be curious about how things look and feel. Have a look at some of your internal landscape.

When you have caught up with your intuition introduce yourselves. Be interested. Find out what it's been up to recently, how it thinks your life is working out. Ask what it will take for the two of you to work together.

This could be a cuddle, a commitment for you to listen, an intention to spend more time together. Be open to what your intuition is telling you!

And then having made your arrangements come away and bring yourself gently but firmly back into the room where you are sitting and in your own time, and when you are ready, open your eyes.

Notice if you sense that anything is different. How are you feeling?

Write down the key points. What did this exercise feel like? What landscape did you look in, what were the colours, and importantly what was the gist of the conversation with your intuition. Did you make any arrangements to work together and what are the arrangements, or what did you agree?

Looking inside is a feature of this book and experimenting with this can be fascinating. This is navel gazing at its best! Our bodies hold vital clues about what is going on for us.

If you have an ache or pain or are holding tension in a particular area of your body find a quiet space and time and close your eyes. Take your attention to the area which aches, or is hurt, or where there is tension. Ask that part of your body what is happening and what is the ache, hurt, tension about.

Be prepared to listen and trust the first answer you get rather than cancel out the answer with a mind thought.

Working with this form of tuning-in to our body is a good first step to holistic awareness.

Within ourselves we are physical, mental, emotional as well a spiritual beings.What is happening on one level, say our mental functioning, will leave an imprint on all of the other levels. In the same way what we perceive on one level, say the physical in this case, can give us clues or answers to what is happening elsewhere.

In this way tuning into our body can help us access answers to day-to-day questions like what is the source of my acne, or why have I got toothache in my bottom left jaw, through to questions like what is my purpose in life, what am I here to experience?

Be Yourself

In the beginning there was sound.

Ohm

Om

Aum

Try it.

If you're feeling a little self-conscious try it in the bathroom or away in the fields or woods where no-one will hear you.

The sound that comes out is right.

We spend so much time and money in the West on education and so many of our children come out of school with the belief that they can't sing, or draw, or dance, or write, or add up. Odd.

So if that is your heritage and baggage let it go. Try forming a sound without pre-judging yourself. There is no judgement. I honour the light and life within you and give yourself permission to do the same.

Fall into a space where there is no judgement. All that exists in this space is the sound you are making. Ohm. Let it reverberate, vibrate. Try closing your eyes and bring the sound out on each out-breath for about 5 minutes.

Notice the sensations. Jot them down in a notebook. If you haven't done so already this is as good a time as any to find a note-book to accompany you on your journey to be yourself.

Most of the spiritual truths that we grapple with are paradoxes.

Example? Well, we have destiny and physics and mediums can foretell, some with astonishing accuracy, what will happen in the future.

And we have freewill. We are told that how things get done on planet earth is by freewill.

How are these reconciled?

Well, it is our destiny to express freewill and in exercising our freewill we express our destiny.

On the surface it sounds like semantics, moving words around.

But think about it for a while…

You have a destiny and that destiny is to do what you want to do. Be who you want to be. You are here because you are here.

Run that by me again. I am here because I am here.

Kiss my arse!

I am that I am.

I need no justification, no philosophy, no label, not nine minutes of fame or celebrity status. I am. I just am!

It's the return of you as an early two year old when you understood, I am that I am. I'm really happy sitting here digging in the sand. Or watching the beetle in the grass. Or just sitting. I'm self-contained.

And then what of you as a more experienced two-year old when you work out you have this freedom but it comes at a price. You can't do this, can't have that, it's not for you?

In adult-speak we might say what of doing and being together, sharing a social contract, family ties, employment, relationships, market-place commerce, intimacy?

How can I watch a good film because who would bother to make one?

And how can I watch a good film with friends and ice-cream and skip down the road afterwards discussing what it was about if everyone has said no, I am that I am?

Because I am is here for the experience of being I am and can only experience that I am-ness in relation to everyone and everything else. If no one was taking any notice how would you know what I am is?

And we relate to each other to help share out how we meet our basic physical and emotional necessities, shelter, food, warmth, love, passion, beauty, joy.

Even if we grow to be adults and then decide we want to be entirely on our own – feasible – we still need others to give us the definition and experience that how we are and what we are experiencing is living alone.

So be it! - for the most marvellous experience you can give to yourself or another is to be yourself.

Be your own wonderful self.

Breathe

If you're breathing it's good news. You're alive. Keep breathing and live longer, live more fully. Let the magic of life fill you up.

Here's a breathing sequence that takes a maximum of three to four minutes to do each day.

You will need to breathe-in wide and full. This means into your stomach as well as your lungs.

Put your hands lightly on the sides of your stomach and feel yourself inflating with an in-breath. Experiment a little with how you breathe and then come back to this sequence a little later if you start to feel dizzy.

Once you have the knack of breathing-in wide and full try breathing in so that one third of your breath goes into your stomach, one third into your lungs and heart area, and one third goes into your shoulders and throat area.[3]

If this is new then take your time to experiment and be comfortable with breathing in thirds before adding the words below.

The sequence is made up of affirmations each of which are repeated three times. So in all you are taking 12 breaths and bringing the air to your stomach, lungs and heart, and shoulders and throat in equal proportions.

I should add you are letting the breath out each time too! And as you do this allow yourself to let go of tension, day-to-day thoughts, and melt or merge into the moment a little.

---

3 With thanks to Ruth Fox who does amazing energy healing for this breathing technique in thirds

With each breath focus on being alive. The breath is life-force or prana, the means to be and exist.

Take your time with this and go at your own pace, the technique or pattern of this will fall into place as you relax.

The sequence goes like this:

Each breath is a miracle of life
Each breath is a miracle of life
Each breath is a miracle of life

With each breath I am a miracle of life
With each breath I am a miracle of life
With each breath I am a miracle of life

Each breath is universal love
Each breath is universal love
Each breath is universal love

With each breath I am universal love
With each breath I am universal love
With each breath I am universal love

If it happens that you have a spare five minutes after this close your eyes and go within yourself:

On the last breath, 'with each breath I am universal love' imagine you are flowing with the breath, into your body, and into your heart where all of this universal love resides.

Settle there, simply be, for 5 minutes, and maybe a while longer if this comes easily to you or once you have the hang of it.

And listen.

Listen

If you're doing this book sequentially then you may have listened without fear or judgement when you were making the sound aum, ohm, om.

Do it now if you have a moment as it's the fastest way to experience what follows:

Let whatever sound you have come out. This is an act of creation.

You may notice that after you have finished making the sound there is a residue. An echo. But after that?

Is it still with you? Not loud but there as something else that you've possibly missed for a while?

It's not the sound of the aum itself it's the sound of the vibration, the sound of the energy being moved and forming new patterns.

Stay with this to see if this comes to you or return when there's not as much background noise or when you don't have to be somewhere else.

It is possible to hear yourself.

You may have come across the expression "I can't hear myself think" which usually describes a state where there's simply too much noise, too much distraction, and the mind is trying to decipher which noise to filter out and which to focus on.

Once the noise has gone then we can hear ourselves think because it's usually the 'sound' of us talking to ourself.

Now take this a step further.

Our thoughts are energy and energy moving can be heard. So close your eyes and think of yourself beating a really large gong or large cymbal. Can you hear the sound?

Now relax and see if the sound you hear is inside your head? If it is it's most likely that you're recreating it from previous memories of the sound. What about if it's outside your head?

Take time with this and return to it if conditions around you currently are not right.

Once you can hear the sound outside your head it opens the possibility in a very physical and also logical way that with our thought we create our world. Our thoughts are powerful. We can hear them.

Try experimenting with other thoughts and the sounds they make. What is the sound of you putting a book down i.e. in your thoughts? What is the sound of you rolling a coin across a table?

We are all composed of energy. Our energy vibrates and makes a sound. What do you sound like? Listen for the sound outside your ears.

Is the sound healthy or does it suggest that there is something out of balance? If there is something out of balance where does this out of balance sound come from and what does it suggest?

It is possible by tuning into the sound of ourselves to know when we have physical, mental, spiritual or emotional imbalance, to know where this is coming from, and to know the nature of the imbalance and how to correct it.

This awareness can be honed and focused so that we have the potential to tune into the sound of insects, trees, plants, as well as ourselves and other people. An example of this was given in the film ‘Ray’, being the story of the musician Ray Charles and Ray demonstrates this ability to a girlfriend.

But why not experiment with this yourself?

Follow your ability to filter out sound and listen for the sound you decide to focus on. It is easier if this is a living and breathing point of reference, like another person, yourself, an animal, a plant or tree as examples.

Listen first to the sounds that you are familiar with. The sound of the breath, the body functioning in other ways, like digestion or your heartbeat etc.

Then listen for the sound which is behind, beyond or is a background sound awareness. Be open to the answers you intuitively know rather than the answers you think you know. This exercise is therefore good for beginning to discriminate between what we know in our mind and what we know as an awareness.

And practice the exercise when you have a spare moment and you’ll find you can hear thought, energy and vibration even in busy or otherwise loud environments.

Separate and one

The answer to everything lies within you because ultimately we are all one. We can express that consciousness separately and collectively.

You are a drop in the ocean and you are the ocean. You are a breath of wind and you are the wind.

If you have time now then experiment with this otherwise come back when you have 5 minutes:

Find a quiet space and time. Suspend any phone calls or external demands. This is fantastic to do in nature like sitting under a tree, so if you have the opportunity to sit outside go for it.

Sit comfortably. Close your eyes and bring your awareness gently to your breath. Breathe in and feel the life-force, the prana, nourishing your body. Breathe out and be conscious of how the breath is re-joining all of the air which is outside your body.

Now breath in for a second time and notice, just before the end of your in-breath, how the air is all connected. It is only the end of the in-breath which causes the disconnection. If you pause at this moment you will find that everything is suspended. All is one, as it always is, and all is separate, as it is, to feed your body.

You take what you need from the whole and you are connected to the whole and return to the whole with each breath.

So it is with water in the ocean. Close your eyes and see a wave. It forms as a distinct and separate shape to the water supporting it below.

On the top of the wave a drop of water is blown by the wind.

It separates and forms a distinct droplet. And then the wind drops and the droplet falls back into the wave and the wave back into the ocean. Separate and together as one.

Being either and being both brings astonishing experiences and knowledge. As a separate being, the sense of what it is to be alone, what it is to be touched by another or loved by another, or shunned by another.

The coming together as one, and what it is to be part of a collective consciousness. You may remember the day on which the news of the death of Diana, Princess of Wales was broadcast in Britain, and the surge and mix of love and grief. Love and grief for Diana for sure, and love and grief for ourselves and for our human condition.

Or being one: the knowledge that what one person has done others can learn from and do also. Fly to the moon, heal others as if miraculously, run a mile in less than 4 minutes or bake a cake which tastes sublime.

Human consciousness is a composite of all human beingness, and is responsive to every thought, word and deed or non-deed on the planet. How we understand ourselves and find ourselves acting or behaving can also be influenced by human consciousness.

This is sometimes referred to as the 100th monkey syndrome: i.e. when a sufficient number of people hold a particular vibration or knowledge they can simultaneously share that knowledge or consciousness with all other humans. Possibly something of this consciousness was shared in eastern Europe in the late 1980's when separation between east and west Europe began to dissolve.

How this is achieved is via energy and thought. How this operates is the subject of the next chapter.

Energy

We are all energy. Some energy is dense and forms into matter, our bodies for instance, or the chair you are sitting on. And some energy is light. Thoughts for instance.

Some thoughts are heavier like anxiety or stress. Others are lighter like happiness and love.

We can surround ourselves with dense thoughts and send out dense thoughts to another, or we can surround ourselves with light and send out light thoughts.

We know from watching the effects of gravity that heavy drags us down, light lifts us up. And what we need as human beings and spiritual beings is balance.

So if something is out of whack change the energy.

This can be what you eat, what you drink, the company you keep, the environment you are in, the thoughts you have about yourself or about others to cite but a few examples.

Did you know that it is impossible to be depressed it you look up? You may not feel like looking up but if you wish to change your mood you can.

If energy is the key be aware of your thoughts and notice how you can change things about you, consciously or unconsciously. This can be simple but profound like how you dress in the morning or how you decide you are going to experience the day.

Getting dressed. Which fabrics and which colours are you drawn to? What does the colour mean for you? If you want something with more energy you may be drawn to red, or orange for happiness, yellow for sunshine or black for efficiency, or deep blue for protection and so on. Choosing a different colour can change your energy and how you experience your day.

With your thoughts you can 'send' energy. Co-operation and clarity to a meeting where you have things to negotiate for instance. Openness and appreciation of collective working if you are working on a project with others and wish to create a climate within which things can get done together.

You can send energy and thoughts anywhere you choose around the world or the universe.

For now you might like to experiment with what this can mean in a way where you can get immediate feedback. Do this with a friend who is in the same room (and then experiment with this when they are in a different room to know this can be done anywhere if you like)

Ask your friend for their permission.

Ensure you're in a quiet time and space. Ask them to close their eyes so that they can tune into any changes in feeling in their energies. Now decide what you wish to send them. Let's say you are sending them a boost of energy. What would this look like? It's maybe warm or quite hot, it can be lots of laughter, or intense and bright light. Say you settle on an intense and bright white light which brings with it unconditional love.

Close your eyes if you wish. Focus on your friend and see white, intense, loving light going from their toes, feet, ankles, up their legs, thighs, groin area, torso, chest, their back, shoulders, arms, up the throat, face, forehead and scalp.

Take this slowly and with fluency of movement so that the thought form flows equally. A bit like slow-motion or maybe just slightly slower but with a consistency of movement.

Ask your friend for feedback.

If follows that we can send each other anxiety and fear, or love and light. We can do this consciously or unconsciously.

Until we decide on a world where we are conscious about how we use such powerful energies it makes sense to protect ourselves.

The energy which cuts through all others is light. The highest vibration of white light is unconditional love so it makes sense to ask for protection of the purest form of unconditional love. You can surround yourself in light of this kind anytime you wish, your thoughts are energy.

The traditional way to do this is to see yourself in a bubble of the purest form of unconditional love. Say like an egg-shape around you. If it feels comfortable form an intention that the light bubble around you transmutes i.e. changes, any stray dense thoughts which come your way.

You are now in a position where you can not only protect yourself from energy which potentially could drag you down but you have the ability to lighten the environment around you whilst you do it.

If your friend is willing you could experiment with different kinds of energy. Laughter for instance is infectious and a good energy to experiment with.

The nugget or jewel in the experiments is the knowledge that by choosing your thoughts and monitoring your thoughts so that they are consistent you can change your experience of life and how you relate to life.

And it follows that it is possible to get together with like minded people and change the environment, community or world in which you live.

What is my life's purpose?

If you are used to jogging along with life, looking after yourself and others as best you can, deciding what your life purpose is can be challenging. We might frame our answers according to how we're used to relating to others: what's right to keep the peace, what fits in with others, what's possible within our budget and so on.

Or possibly what's right for us according to who we have been in the habit of thinking we are. I'm this kind of person, with this kind of background, these kinds of qualifications for instance.

But all of this can change if you wish it to.

We are all energy and our thoughts are energy. Just as you can change the way in which your friend is feeling by sending them energy and you can change the way in which you experience your life by monitoring your thoughts, you can also bring your life into line with your truth about yourself.

How do you do this?

There are many ways to find out who you are and what your life purpose is. For instance.

<u>How do you come over to other people?</u>
Ask friends and family to write down a sentence or phrase which they feel sums you up. Ask 10 people and look at what reaction you get when you read or hear the sentences they give you. Trust your intuition i.e. your gut feeling rather than your logical mind. Your mind may wish to take you to answers which you feel comfortable with because you had already decided that about yourself, what you are after are those which speak to your truth. You'll know it in your gut. Not because it says nice and

comfortable things about you but because you'll know it's right. It's your awareness or intuition.

Ask to be read.
You can ask people who have the gift or have studied how to 'read' other people. This can be people who read the lines on your hand; or interpret the date, time and place of your birth and then study the alignment of planets which match those factors; or people who read your psychic energy field, or who listen to energy which is external to you, say spirit for shorthand, and are able to tell you who you are. All or any of these methods and others besides can be astonishingly accurate.

Or you can go within.
Here's how to go within if this appeals to you.

Find a quiet time and space. Allow yourself 20 minutes for reflection and maybe 10 minutes to write things up afterwards.

Find a candle which will be safe to use for the exercise. Light the candle, sit comfortably and focus on the flame of the candle.

Begin to see four kinds of colour in the flame. You have gold, silver, violet and the most pure white.[4]

Now close your eyes and see the image of this flame in front of you. In your imagination enlarge the flame until it is life-size and walk into it, letting it envelope you. Stay here a couple of minutes and get used to the energy. It can be very direct and freeing. You may feel a cleansing or purification at this point. That's fine.

---

[4] I am taking the gold, silver and violet flame from the work of Diana Cooper. There are qualities and energies which are associated with the colours and for further details on this visit Diana's website at www.dianacooper.com where you also have the option of sending a flame to other people or situations.

Now in your imagination see only the pure white of the flame at the very centre. Enter into the white flame and feel it all around you. Within the flame there is a chair or a bench for you. Sit on it and allow yourself to feel who you are.

Simply allow this experience to be as it is.

When you have become accustomed to the energy within the white flame and to the sense of yourself, ask who am I, and what is my life's purpose?

Listen or sense an answer or a feeling or indeed a set of feelings. Honour your own awareness and let it be as it is.

Allow yourself 10 to 15 minutes within the pure white flame for this and come back into your physical self by returning the way that you went. So step backwards from the white flame and feel the gold, silver and violet flame around you. Next step backwards from this flame and see yourself outside the candle flame image that you started with.

Then when you are ready bring yourself gently but firmly back into your physical space feeling your feet on the floor and your bum on your physical chair and wriggle your toes and fingers and gently open your eyes.

When you are ready write down what you felt. Without wishing to make suggestions - each of us is individual and will experience this exercise differently - feel for the awareness which is you. It may be deeply peaceful, or loving, or simply very familiar in a way that you've not experienced for some time.

Extending this exercise you can begin to ask **what serves my purpose**? Are you living your life consciously, or putting up with things, or doing things out of habit?

There follows an exercise to get us in touch with what serves our purpose.

Find a quiet space and time and provide yourself with paper and a pencil or pen. Allow up to 30 minutes without interruptions if possible. Find somewhere to sit or lie comfortably. Tune into the feelings you had when you journeyed into the flame and into your inner awareness to know who you are and what your life's purpose is. Allow this feeling to be at your core. Close your eyes to get back to this feeling if it helps.

Now start writing in two columns

What serves my purpose?

This does not serve my purpose	This does serve my purpose
To be treated disrespectfully	To respect myself
To neglect my children or see them limited by lack of love	To love my children freely and without condition
To leave myself short of time so that I am unprepared for the day	To allow time for me
To live hand-to-mouth never being sure how I will pay the next large bill	To allow abundance into my life so that I may be supported in being who I truly am
To have relationships with others where I feel I am not expressing freely and truthfully who I am	To be me to be free

As you can see the examples here mirror each other to a large extent so that not wanting to be treated disrespectfully starts with respecting ourself and setting that as our intention for others. In this way what you know does not serve your purpose can be defined by what you have already experienced or what you have observed as the experience of others. It is also possible to construct a list in a single column without bouncing off the counter experience. Something like:

What serves my purpose?

- To acknowledge fully who I am
- To allow myself to be
- To chose each day and in each moment those thoughts and actions which serve my purpose

Other ways of describing what is happening when we focus on our purpose and what serves our purpose are to be ‘inwardly directed’ or to be ‘living in the moment’. These can be felt and experienced once we have tuned in to our own inner-self and inner awareness.

To choose and to do this consciously brings us back to questions about what we believe about ourselves. It is for more discussion about these concepts that we turn in the next chapter.

Self-belief

Our beliefs about ourselves come from a variety of sources. It's possible that few of these beliefs have basis in your truth or have much relevance to what your life purpose is.

Take a piece of paper and write on the left side 'what I believe about myself', and on the right 'where this belief came from':

What I believe about myself	Where this belief came from
I'm good at cooking	my mum
I'm rubbish at football	boys at school

Then once you're past the surface of things go a little deeper. Are you a compassionate person; do you take responsibility for your life or tend to blame others; how do you handle anger; do you have fears and what are they and how do you handle them; how do you handle love, both giving and receiving?

Our self-belief could be represented by a triangle. In day-to-day life this triangle might be spinning and the movement of the triangle represents the three points in motion, which then supports the core or axis. At the three points we have thought, word and deed and these support our core self-belief which is the point on which the triangle can spin i.e. the axis.

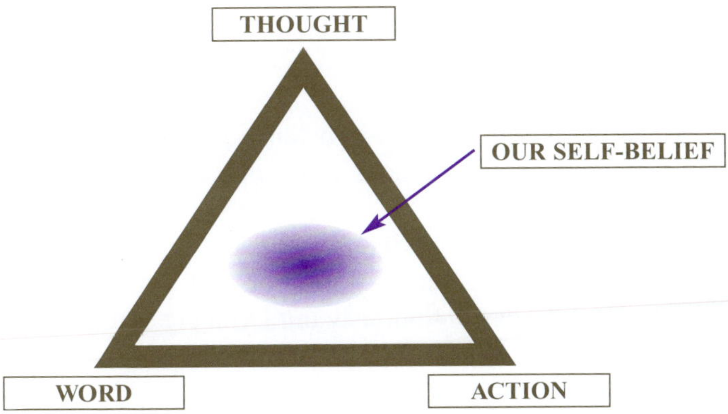

On a day-by-day basis it is possible to change our self-belief by changing any or all of the energies at the three points i.e. what you think, what you say and what you do.

This may depend on how much time you give yourself for reflection before thought appears. For example…you have a belief about yourself that you are not worthwhile and you are therefore slow to put boundaries around your time or meeting your priorities when others are looking for your help. A friend asks you for a lift on the way home from work which you know will take you out of your way and slow or even change plans you had for the evening.

It could be your triangle starts spinning out of habit into words “well, yes of course I’ll give you a lift, no problem”, even though your thoughts may be in conflict with this or possibly haven’t had time to assess the situation.

It could be your actions are out of synchronicity. Your mouth says yes and then later in the day you develop an illness so have to go home early. Other possibilities are that you look for an authority which you feel will be more acceptable than your wishes. So you find extra work to be done (your boss asks you).

In these kinds of examples it’s likely your triangle is wobbling i.e. your core self-belief is out of tune with who you are and what your purpose is and your thoughts, words and deeds are therefore out of balance.

To get the triangle to spin in balance you can tackle each of the three points and bring them into synchronicity.

This means changing what you think, say or do. For this to be effective you will need to monitor and patrol your thoughts, words and deeds continuously until you are sure your self-belief has changed.

And/or you can change your core belief.

<u>Changing your core belief</u>

Take a fresh sheet of paper. Write down your beliefs about yourself in a column on the left. Opposite these beliefs a column indicating where these came from. Decide if the belief serves your purpose.

If yes underline or highlight the belief on your paper and resolve to tune into more of this quality and bring it more into your life.

If you find the belief does not serve you you may hand it back to the person who first suggested it to you.

Find a quiet space and time. Close your eyes. Ask the person who gave you this belief to stand before you and say gently but firmly, "I no longer wish to use this belief. It is not mine. Thankyou." And hand it back. Say goodbye, give the person a hug if this feels appropriate and leave.

It could be there are many people who have helped to confirm a self-belief which you now know is not who you are and does not serve your purpose:

Find a quiet space and time. Sit or lie comfortably. Close your eyes and bring all of the people you need to hand back this belief to before you. Make a small ceremony of this if you wish. Decide on a form of words which honestly reflects who you are:

"Thankyou all for coming. Thanks for the belief which you have held collectively about me. This belief has served me up until now but is no longer who I am. I therefore hand it back to you all. Namasté"

Once the core belief is changed the triangle which supports it changes too.

Change is possible because we can choose how we experience life on earth. This is freewill.

Things which often appear to be opposites and are seen as being in opposition to each other for instance freewill versus destiny, or plenty versus scarcity can also live in harmony with each other where there is a third and equal point of reference. This is the principle which leads to the question, have we found the holy grail? and this is the subject of the next section.

Part Two: Adventure

- What is the holy grail?
- Duality
- Trinity
- Is this the holy grail?
- Experience grail energies
- The balance of paradox

Part two is the adventure of the grail.

Not the physical adventure of raiding the temple of doom or the will we - won't we - suspense of vanquishing hidden forces. More an armchair adventure into the nature of yourself.

As they say in all good books, suspend your disbelief for a moment that a journey into the nature of yourself is capable of providing lots of adventure, and read on.

What is the holy grail?

There's a few books on the holy grail which have been published recently, as well as some classics on the subject. Mark Amaru Pinkham in "Guardians of the Holy Grail" gives a summary of the literature and openly accessible information about the grail.[5]

Physically the grail is described as a cup or chalice; possibly a spear; or maybe the philosopher's stone or a variation of something equally solid. This could be the embalmed head of John the Baptist or John the Apostle or both.

The 'V' shape of the chalice might signify the womb, and the birth of children, in the case of the grail energies the descendants of Jesus Christ and Mary Magdalene which began with their daughter Sarah or Tamar.[6]

There are holy relics and sacred or magical objects which are associated with grail energies. These include wooden fragments of the cross on which Jesus Christ was crucified, the shroud in which Jesus was wrapped for burial and the sword in the stone of Arthurian legend amongst others.

The grail appears to be a vehicle for energies which bring the gift of immortality, profound healing and spiritual understanding. Where the grail appears as a symbol i.e. the chalice represents a 'V' the energies associated with the symbol have something of the same properties i.e. they bring healing and insights of a profound spiritual nature.

The grail legends have been in circulation either as oral or written spiritual adventure for at least 3,200 years and therefore

---

[5] "Guardians of the Holy Grail" by Mark Amaru Pinkham. Published by Adventures Unlimited Press. 2004.

[6] The history and teachings of Mary Magdalene, including the story of the birth of Jesus and Mary is written up in " The secret Gospel of Mary Magdalene"

pre-date Christianity and the birth and times of Jesus Christ - the figure with whom the legends are most usually associated with in the West.

The legends also appear to be largely gnostic in character i.e. of themselves they do not lend authority to any one religion or way of thinking but speak to everyone and bring a universal energy which can be received by anyone or everyone in their heart.

From this brief summary of grail legend the discussion within this book proceeds on the basis that the grail is here with us and it is hidden from view or is overlooked. It also feels as though it is symbolic rather than physical in nature and the 'V' symbol is important.

The energies which the grail brings are formidable and will deliver heaven on earth if that is what we choose.

By focusing and living with things which appear to be opposites i.e. freewill versus destiny or plenty versus scarcity we live within narrow confines. It is by lifting the line on duality and creating a new dimension within which our true nature may be revealed that we understand the grail energy.

The nature of things being in opposition, duality, and things being in balance, trinity, is discussed over the next two chapters so that we can arrive at a consideration of the grail where new possibilities about ourselves, about new energies, and about new dimensions can be considered.

Duality

Duality is a spectrum in which each end of the line is held by things which appear to be in opposition.

Some examples of opposites which are held to be convenient for understanding our experience in human form are:

hot and cold

light and dark

short and tall

life and death

rich and poor

love and fear

aggression and peace

masculine and feminine

Duality is a convenient means of gaining experience. What is light if we don't know dark? What is love if we have no experience of a convenient opposite. In this case fear ?

Reading through this list you may have questions. For instance, poor and rich are relative terms and carry judgements with them. In common day use rich is largely a judgement about material resource i.e. money or environment and does not necessarily include considerations such as physical health, or emotional well-being, or spiritual understanding.... indeed many of the things, say if we have poor health or if we know ourselves to be close to death, things which we identify as important to us and our quality of life.

There are other things in the list which do not stand-up to cursory questions. What of life and death? Is it one or the other or does our physical death transform this life into something that is not the opposite of life in human form but a continuation of life in a different form?

And if you believe in karma and our ability to re-incarnate is the line of opposition more likely to be a circle?

The discussion about masculine and feminine is picked up later in part two. For now it can be noted that in joining masculine and feminine energy together, in love or as observed biological fact, the two energies become one. This is in the act of making love, and in the joining of the egg and the sperm to make one. The one becomes a third. Life, creation.

mother father

I

Is it the case that the principle of a third and equal point of reference exists in all of our polarities?

Each of our polarities suggest there is something other going on otherwise they are simply a line on a page or an abstract concept. What if what is missing is life itself? What if this means experience, relationship, relativity, dimension?

<u>Dimension</u>

Two lines give us a cross on which we can hang ourself or an opportunity to create a new dimension. Take an image of two cheese strings or maybe strands of dna which, laid horizontally are flat and provide a polarity. Once one of these is picked up and formed into a different shape there is an opening through which another dimension can be felt and experienced.

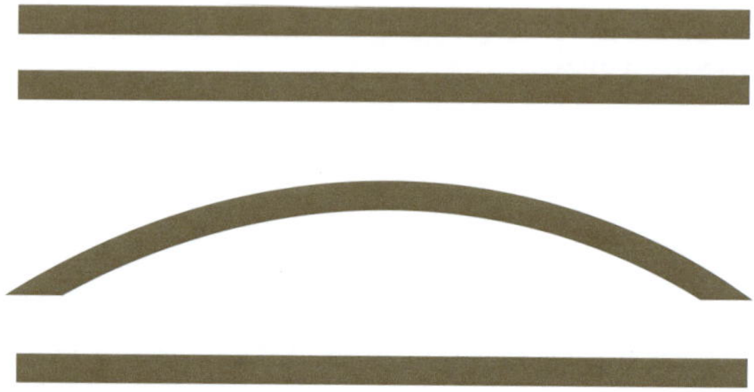

It is a sense of dimension which arrives with having three points rather than two which provides a point at which life can enter and through which things can be understood.

And what if life and dimension provide the keys to understanding where to find the grail and grail energies?

To progress this discussion it may help to look in more detail at the nature of trinity.

Trinity

The proposition that a trinity is a key to the grail follows on from a discussion with friends of mine, Harry Owen and Omar Rafiqi. Harry was sure that the grail was comprised of a trinity in nature and Omar wondered if the trinity was always present but simply obscured by our focus on the nature of duality.

There is also a triangle from Vernon Frost which carries the vibration of unconditional love and which brings with it healing energies.[7]

For the purposes of this discussion this triangle can represent a gift of eternal peace on earth. The gift is from your god i.e. universal love, source, all that is, God, Allah.

The energies within this triangle are formidable and are capable of assisting healing and clarity of mind and purpose if you choose to use them or experience them in this way.

[7] Vernon Frost is a metaphysical teacher who is based in South Africa and who travels to facilitate workshops in the UK amongst other destinations. See Ruth Fox's website at www.adventuresinconsciousness.co.uk for further details

When we choose to focus on duality we can loose sight of the trinity. For instance, the opposite of unconditional love is conditional love

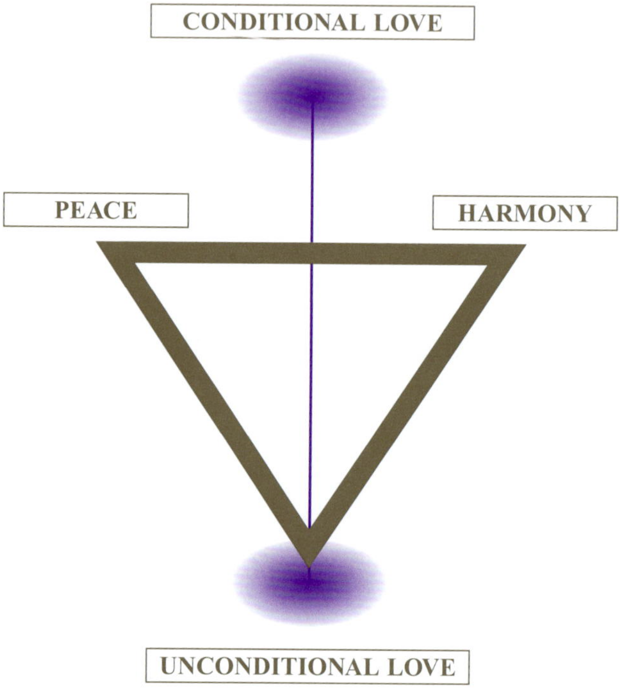

The diagram begins to resemble the sword in the stone. The eternal truth, represented by the stone, never went away. All that happened was that we lost sight of it and became misled by the pull of conditional love.

If we take any of the other points on the triangle we can similarly set up an opposition which compromises our ability to see the triangle in daily life because our focus is on the points where we allow fear room to grow. For instance the opposite of peace may be anxiety or similarly harmony by discord

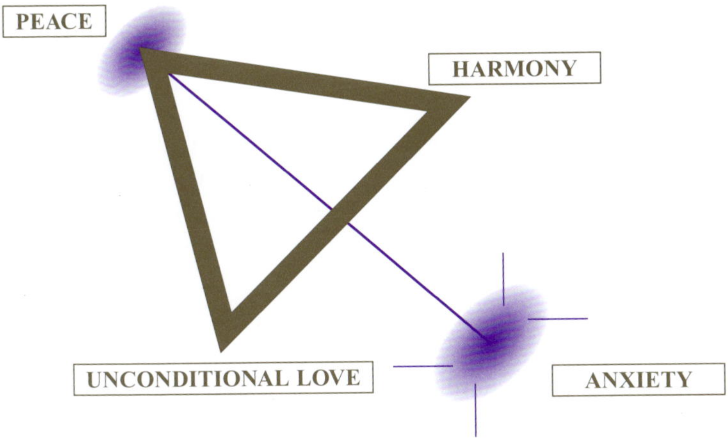

Does this triangle work for other values? For instance peace and harmony might hold an axis along two points with a third point of reference holding a value. For instance justice:

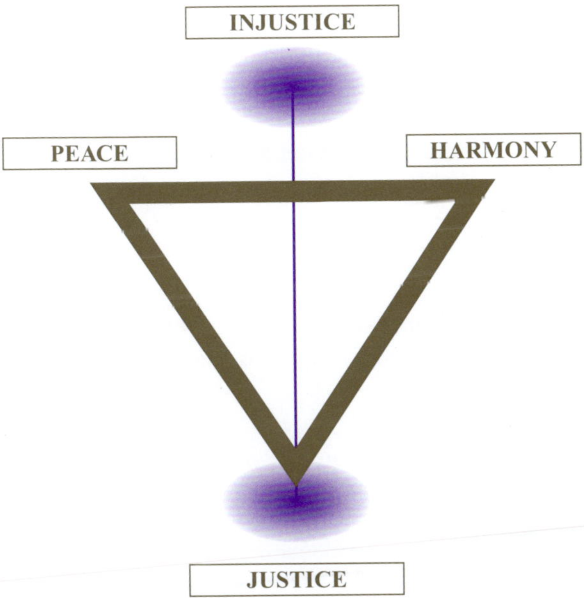

Is it the case that we live in a narrow dimension because of a focus on opposites, in this case justice and injustice, and miss a dimension which is balanced?

Similar triangles can be overlooked. What about plenty or abundance being opposed by scarcity rather than seeing the gift of universal support, or where compassion is countered by anger or guilt?

If there is mileage in conceptually having three points and being able to create a dimension into which we can step then the triangle will need to be capable of reinterpreting many life experiences which otherwise might pass for duality in western cultures[8] and also be a triangle in which we can live, breathe and experience.

From the example above it appears to follow that what we see as duality disguises the triangle. Let's try light as illumination and dark, the absence of light:

In polarity and opposition they can be portrayed or conceptualized as holding opposite ends of a straight line or spectrum.

However, do we miss other points of reference?

---

[8] I am generalising about culture and belief to illustrate the point and may have strayed into caricature.

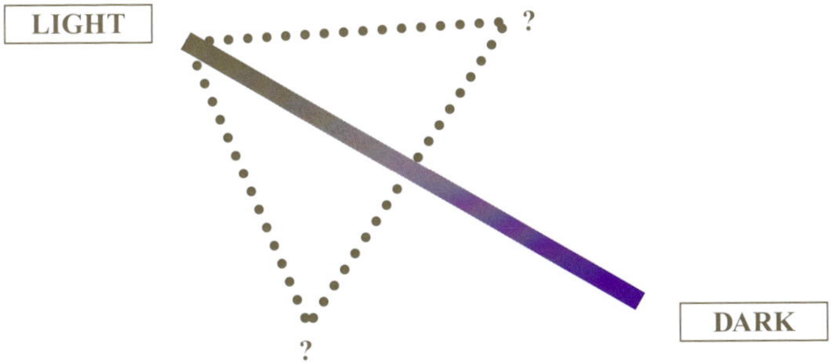

Dark here can be held in peace and harmony as with values like justice and compassion. But surely it is the blend of the two opposites which creates our experience?

If this is the case then our trinity might look different in terms of the principles by which it is constructed.. It becomes something like

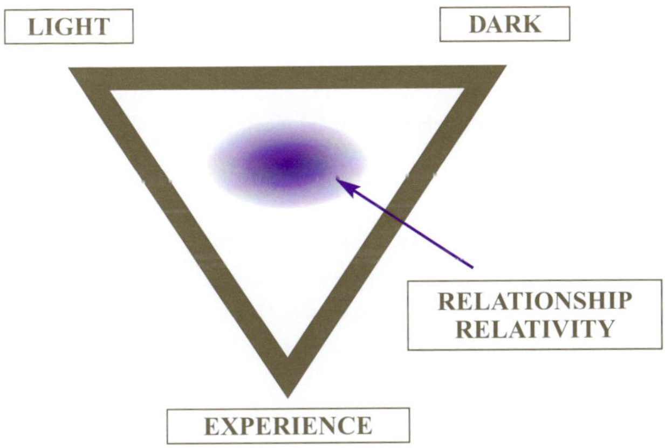

In this triangle experience is shorthand for the dimension provided by relationship, relativity and life itself to happen. In

this way the triangle works for things we seek to experience such as short and tall, hot and cold, and concepts which are said to be in opposition like freewill versus destiny.

If the triangle provides a shape for the grail, and from the shape certain principles which can inform how we live, how do we do it. i.e. how do we live within this triangle and how do we access this energy?

Stepping into something requires more action and more involvement. It's an act of being in the moment, being conscious, being life, when compared to sliding along a line between two positions which are said to be in opposition.

<u>As above so below</u>

If we have a triangle from spirit what about something which matches that energy which can be created here on earth and which provides an experience to which we can all relate here on earth?

The presence of a triangle on earth is certain once we accept the principle that what exists above i.e. in heaven, is also reflected on earth. As above so below which is one of the universal truths or laws.[9]

Our eternal triangle is the diagram of peace, love and harmony.

An earth triangle would need to reflect these aspects. Peace and harmony allow us to be in the flow.

Reflections of peace and harmony on earth might be giving and receiving. Kahlil Gilbran in "The Prophet" reminds us that we are all receivers and letting love and joy be received is an

---

[9] This is cited in a number of sources, but for a discussion of this and other spiritual laws see Diana Cooper's "A little light on the spiritual laws" by Hodder & Stoughton

ability which many people are having to learn.

If you are in any doubt about how much love you choose to receive close your eyes and tune into your heart and ask your heart.

Giving i.e. attention, smiles, happy thoughts, care, love, resource, is the other side of the polarity.

Where the dimension with receiving and giving might be found is in honouring. This is in seeing the creator, source, all that is, universal love, in each and every one of us. This includes plants, trees, crystals, animals, fish, birds etc in fact anything that has an energy or auric field.

Honouring is seeing or acknowledging and then saluting the spirit or light in all of us. We are separate and we are one. Or Namasté for short.

If the triangle exists as evidence of the grail then as with the eternal triangle there will be an energy with this triangle which we can feel or sense. The energy will allow for healing to take place and within the energy you can move around and breathe.

As with the eternal triangle the proof of the theory will be in experimenting with the energy.

To do this find a quiet space and time. Close your eyes. Focus on each of the points of the triangle separately for a minute or so each and then see if the energy around the triangle begins to move in a way in which you can sense i.e. feel, see, hear.

If giving, receiving and honouring are proving abstract as concepts, focus on your heart and ask to grow your triangle from your heart. i.e. start small and then let the triangle get bigger until it covers most of the area of your torso. And then let it grow again until it is your size or larger and you can feel yourself within the energy.

If imaging is something that doesn't come naturally to you then take a different approach. Think of someone who you regard as a role model in your life.

Let this person be who they are i.e. someone who was important to you because of the love and care they brought into your life in whatever form.

Focus on this person and feel the effect of receiving the qualities, the love, for which you remember them at this moment. Now see how this makes you feel in terms of giving. Close your eyes and feel what it is you would like to give back to this person. A hug perhaps or to say thankyou.

Now take the feelings this person has inspired in you and honour the spirit within them. The spark or wave of unconditional love which they brought into your life. Get a sense of how this love, this light, is a part of them but also a part of you.

You are separate and you are one. It is the same love the same light. We choose to experience it in different ways and for experience we separate, but that does not mean we are disconnected. A new triangle begins to take shape with three points being you, experience, and all that is.

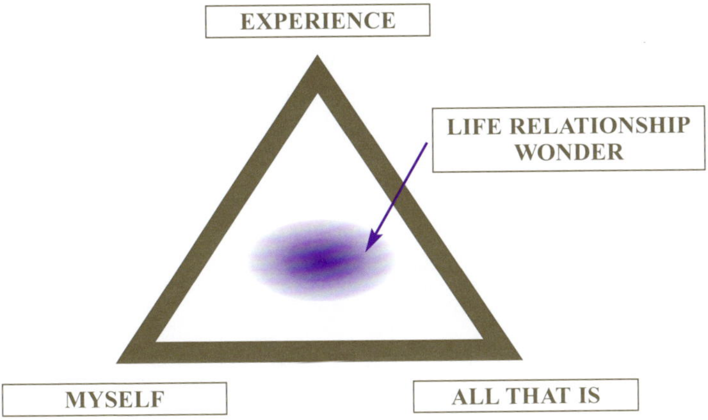

Does this love and this light you are feeling and building extend to other things? The flowers. Your favourite tree. Other significant people in your life? Experiment with it.

Is this the holy grail?

If trinity is the nature of the grail have we found the grail and the grail energy within our triangles?

To develop the discussion we will need to use our senses. Can you feel this energy? Can you live and breathe it? In the discussion so far it is proposed that we have an eternal or spirit triangle which is a balance of peace, harmony and unconditional love

It is proposed that there is a matching trinity on earth according to the principle of 'as above so below' and in keeping with an understanding that the grail energy represents heaven on earth.

An 'earth' triangle might take account of our separation and unity, our freewill and destiny, our desire to connect with God or universal love in each and every one of us, and our sense that our natural state is to 'be in the flow'.

Along the axis of giving and receiving we are learning to open our hearts. To each other and to ourselves. This is to be in the flow and to open to our truth that life is playful, love, experience, beauty, humour, wonder, joy.

Giving and receiving alone might be flat and squashed concepts until we see the light in ourselves and each other. This gives us a dimension within which we can bring these qualities to life, an energy within which we can live and breathe.

If our eternal and our earth triangle mirror each other it is likely that the energies will complement each other. If this stands up then the triangles might also provide a bridge between spirit and matter.

Making a bridge between spirit and matter

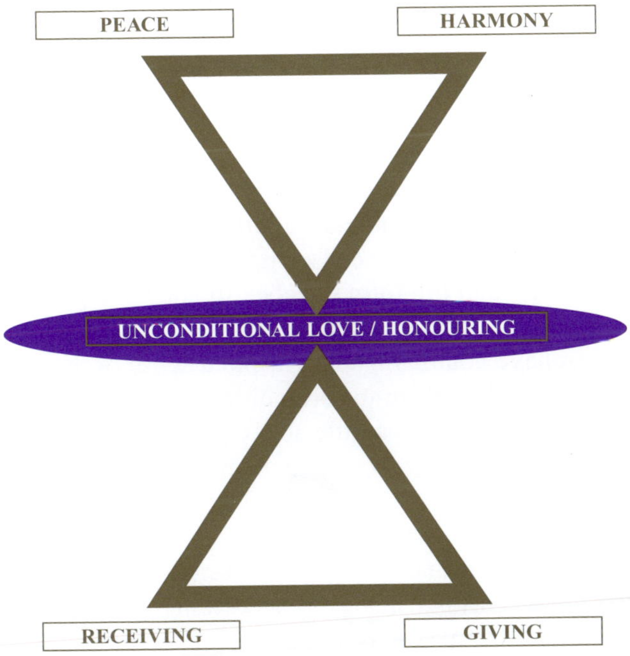

Make this bridge yourself and see how you experience the energy.

Find a quiet space and time where you can close your eyes for about five minutes. Ask source or your understanding of the purest form of unconditional love to form an eternal triangle where peace and harmony are made manifest and given a dimension by unconditional love. This is suspended just above you.

Now form an earth triangle by accepting the flow of love on earth, and receiving and giving love so that there is an equal flow whilst honouring the gift of life.

If you find this hard to imagine or sense then open the palm of your left hand and imagine or feel love coming through this palm, and the same love flowing from your right palm. Your open palms form the bottom of your triangle. If nothing is coming simply hold the thoughts as intentions in your palms and see what you experience.

You will need a dimension into which you can step and live and breathe and this is provided by your third and equal point of reference. This is you honouring life. Seeing universal love, source, creation in everyone else and everything else and let the honour you give to life form the apex to your triangle.

When you have your earth triangle and a sense of the eternal or spirit triangle allow them to 'bridge' in the space in which they are held just in front and a little above you. You may find that at the point at which they touch there is a 'frisson' or spark of energy.

You may also find that your psychic senses i.e. your gifts and abilities as a spiritual being are becoming stimulated at this point. That's fine. You may notice the palms of your hand are hot, or your third eye i.e. the point midway between your physical eyes which is located a little higher up in your brow or forehead begins to tingle.

If this is working and you want to experiment with this further allow the triangles to touch at the points where unconditional love and honouring meet. Notice what is happening for you and how these energies feel.

If the energy feels comfortable the next step is to ask and see the triangles merge.

The merged triangles form a space and an energy vortex within which profound healing can take place. They also form a shape and symbol which is important and carries value for many people via religion and belief systems.

The energy which is available via the process of merging the two triangles might be described as making the energy real and actual i.e. a spiritual actualisation.

When the triangles are merged the energies can be experienced in a variety of ways. They can be applied to the chakras which is a form of healing practiced by Natalie Jayne Ashwood amongst others called 'rising star'.[10]

The merged triangles can provide a space for healing within which a person or people can sit. i.e. you create a physical space large enough to place a chair within. If this feels comfortable try it for yourself.

Have six objects with which you can physically create a space for two triangles. Use objects which of themselves will either enhance the energies available (say like candles, but make sure they are safe to use) or coloured spots drawn on paper.

Create the triangles so that initially they are separate and put an object at each point of the triangle you are making and be aware of the properties which each point is representing i.e. peace, harmony, and unconditional love on the eternal triangle, and giving, receiving and honouring on the earth triangle.

Now merge your triangles physically by moving the objects so that you create a six-pointed star. Move into the space you have created and see how you experience the energy.

My advice is to ask for energies for the highest good. So far as I am aware there are no limitations on what can be achieved or requested in these spaces if the request is for your highest good or the highest good of others.

Once you have experimented with these energies extend the range of how they might be used. They can be created around any physical space. Where you sit to meditate for instance.

---

[10] So far as I am aware 'Rising Star' healing uses similar energies.

Where you eat. Around the home you live in. Your place of work. Around a street, or village or larger community.

And what of working with others to create these energies?

Experience grail energies

In this chapter the grail energy and grail principles which have emerged in previous chapters are transferred and adopted for use with other energies. This is an opportunity to see how portable the principles are and if they point to a new understanding of energies which are currently available to us.

In human or mammal form we take a male seed and a female egg. Points I and 2 on a triangle. They join together to create one which is also point 3 and separate.

New life, new energy. Separate and whole.

This is the joining of male and female energies to create a third which takes a masculine or feminine form.

However. What if the new energies which are created in grail energy are both masculine and feminine? What if the new energy is balanced?

Everything about the grail points to balance. Our concepts are not simply tipped from one point to another they are not one thing or the other or a composite or compromise position.

Mary Magdalene, a spiritual teacher, healer and guide, has popped up a lot in the last few years. There are many books on the subject of her lost years and the systematic downgrading of her 'good name' including the lost teachings of Mary. If you feel a connection with Mary Magdalene then sense which books draw you and read up on this remarkable woman.

And/or you may connect with Mary to form your own experience and understanding

If this sounds attractive then find a quiet space and time. Light a candle. Close your eyes.

You are standing on grass. Feel the grass underneath your feet and your connection with nature. You are being drawn to a rose garden which is a little way in the distance. Move towards it. Notice all of the sensations. Enter the garden.

The roses are grown in fabulous ways. Some form pathways, some ramble, some grow up and over structures which form arbours and bowers with seating where you can sit and meditate.

Roses are symbols of the heart and the heart chakra. With each rose you see you are receiving a drop of unconditional love which enters your heart and sends gentle ripples of love through your heart and throughout your body.

You are being drawn to a path which you follow. Notice the colours. Along your path there is a bench. Around the bench there are hundreds of roses which provide a fabulous fragrance.

Someone is sitting on the bench. It is Mary Magdalene. If it feels right give her a hug. Sit down with her. Ask any questions you may have and sense her energies.

Allow this to be. We have waited for the return of Mary's energies for some time!

When you feel that you have met and become re-acquainted prepare to depart. If it feels right thank Mary. Give her a hug.

Retrace your steps through the rose garden knowing you can come back to this garden any time that you choose. Find yourself outside the garden and back on the grass where you started.

Now bring yourself consciously back into your physical body.

Notice how you are lying or sitting. Wriggle your toes and fingers and gently but firmly open your eyes. Have a drink of water and stretch and yawn.

Record your meeting with Mary in your journal and note down your impressions and sense of your conversation. You may find that things were said between you telepathically i.e. you just know or are aware of what was said.

If you feel a little ungrounded (i.e. spacey) go for a walk physically especially if you can walk in nature.

It felt like Mary's energies were with us over Easter 2007 in particular. It feels as if Mary has re-emerged because it is time to acknowledge that spiritual truth, the grail, is available to all of us, and it is accessible to all of us by going within.

Experiencing the light of the grail

When Jesus, a spiritual teacher, healer and guide, and Mary joined together on earth 2,000 years ago they gave birth to new life. Recent research suggests the new life is a daughter called Sarah or Tamar or possibly there was more than one daughter. In the development of the discussion here the detail is not as important as the bold outline which is the joining of male and female energies.

Let's say that Jesus and Mary represent a form of the eternal triangle. They have joined together at points 1 and 2 to create a 3rd point of reference, a joining together which is one and the creation of something new which is three. Separate and one.

Let's say as above so below and that on earth male and female earth energies have joined together. It may be distracting to give names to these energies and on the other hand it may help.

Let's identify the earth female energy as originating with Lady Gaia, and the earth masculine energy as originating with Sanat Kumara. Let's propose that these energies merged around Easter 2007 to create one which is also a third. A new balanced energy.

This gives us a triangle of eternal truth and an earth triangle which are balanced between male and female polarities. The balance occurs because in combining the energy the act of creation makes one and also a third, a new energy.

These triangles can form a bridge between spirit and matter. This is the lesson from the grail. They look for a portal through which that can happen.

Aha! You are a portal and you may be open to receiving these new energies.

If you are new to experiencing energy or working with energies then turn to the exercise in the first chapter of the next section which is 'grounding, connecting, cleansing and protecting' and do the exercise there first. The exercise is designed to bring into operation your chakras. Chakras are energy points within the body. The term chakra and energy point is being used here interchangeably.

Be comfortable with opening your chakras or energy points before doing the exercise which is described below.

The new energy from earth, the joining together of feminine and masculine energies from Lady Gaia and Sanat Kumara has created a new, balanced energy. Let us call this new energy Saul.

You decide if you are comfortable about this new energy. You will know about this intuitively. If you are not sure then take a step back and take no action on what follows.

If you are comfortable then find a quiet space and time where you will not be disturbed. Sit comfortably. Close your eyes.

Make a thought to connect with the earth and send down roots all the way to the earth's core.

Ask that this new energy, Saul, moves gently up through your roots and up your chakras. Feel this move through the chakras in your feet, your knees, your root chakra (at the base of your spine) and your sacral (located about two finger-widths below your navel) and your solar plexus (top of your stomach) into your heart, your throat chakra, your third eye and up through your crown.

Let this new energy move gently through your energy system and from the crown of your head flow gently too into your energy or auric field.

Now take your awareness to the crown of your head and from your crown move up to connect with your higher self (yourself as a spiritual being about 18 inches above your head) and to connect with your spiritual guides and to connect specifically with Jesus Christ and Mary Magdalene.

If you feel comfortable ask that the energy which has joined and combined, masculine and feminine making one and a separate and new balanced energy in the form of Sarah, move gently down through your energy centres, your chakras, and down through the connection you have with earth, your roots, into the earth's core.

At this point you are acting as a bridge between spirit and matter and helping to anchor, make real, a wonderful new form of energy. See how it feels.

If this feels good then ask that the new energy from the earth,

Saul, move from the earth's core up your energy system, your chakras, to your heart, but no further for the moment.

To match this ask that the new energy from spirit, Sarah, descend through your chakra system to meet with Saul in your heart.

In your heart the two balanced energies merge and combine, Saul and Sarah, to create one new energy, which is one but also separate, a third.

Let us call the new energy Gandana.

The name is a handle, something by which the identity of the energy can be known. It is a new light, a new energy. This new energy, Gandana, combines peace, harmony, unconditional love, giving, receiving and honouring.

Because the grail brings with it a new dimension this energy is something which you can step into.... a space in which you can live and breathe your truth.

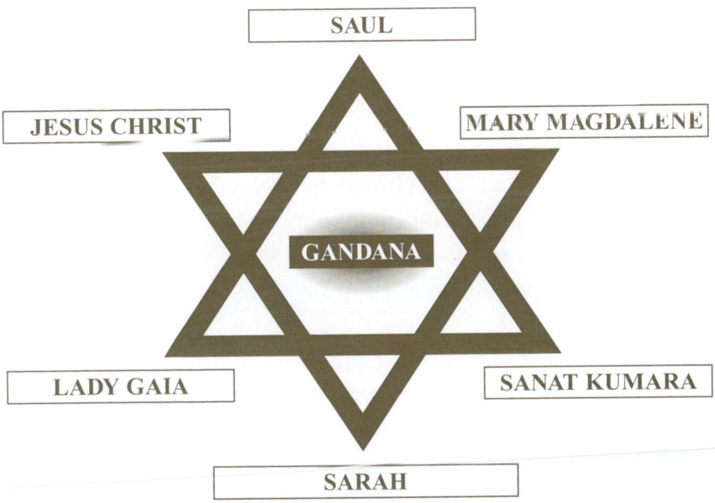

The balance of paradox

Paradox is living with two things which apparently contradict each other. Freewill and destiny is an example. Freewill is how things get done on earth. We chose from moment to moment, depending on the options open to us and our understanding.

Destiny on the other hand appears to be the choices we made before we incarnated. The parents we are born to, the major relationships in our life, the major life events from which we wish to experience. All of these choices can be changed or altered to a substantial degree including our decision to stay around in human form.

Because everything is energy and everything has a vibration we continually attract events and people, relationships and issues, which help us to manifest our choices and bring to us the experiences which we came to earth for.

These vibrations and these choices can be read by others and similarly divined by ourselves if we choose. When reading, or more accurately tuning-in to this vibrational frequency we are able to foretell events and are able to sketch our future.

In this way we live-out destiny and freewill. It's our destiny to express freewill and our choice in freewill to experience our destiny. Holding and living what appears on the surface to be a paradox becomes more manageable when we look for a third point of reference.

The experience of looking for the grail energy suggests that the energy resides in a space where there are three points of reference, a trinity, rather than a simple pull or push sequence of two things which appear to be in opposition.

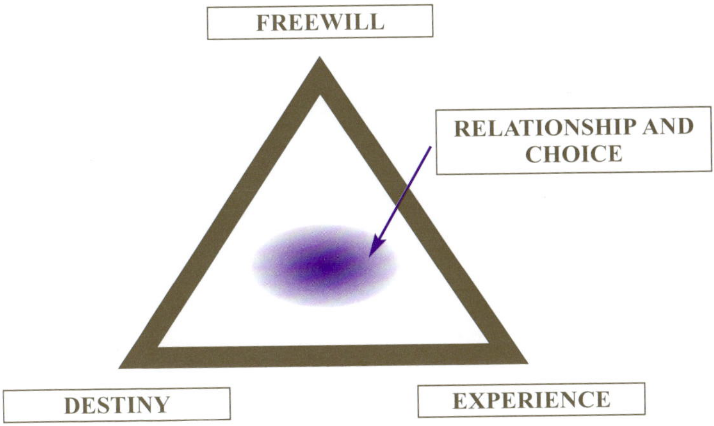

In this example freewill and destiny are balanced by a point of reference which is experience. Experience is common to both. There will be other properties which are common to both. The environment in which life is lived, other people, or the timetable and lifespan for instance. However, the defining characteristic of a third point of reference which brings duality into a new dimension is that the point of reference is of equal value to the first two and provides relationship and experience of life.

Life is therefore not about freewill, or destiny, or experience, but all three at the same time.

And if this feels 'right' as a concept for understanding life, you may notice that life begins to be harmonious, peaceful and full of love.

Part Three: A new way of being

- Ground, connect, cleanse and protect
- Open your heart
- Be the grail energies
- Go direct
- Living through your heart
- Conclusion

In part three it is proposed that we have found the grail and that within the grail energy a new way of being is emerging.

This new way of being will be defined by your truth i.e. whatever you choose and however you wish to be. This includes bringing in heaven on earth in a way which is sustainable.

To do this it is likely that we will develop different dimensions. To experience ourselves differently, to experience relationship with others differently, and to experience our relationship with spirit differently.

Some of the ways to do this we know, some of the ways to do this we will learn from each other, and some of these ways we will develop between us.

Ground, connect, cleanse and protect

We are all energy and can connect and disconnect from each other at will. We are separate and we are one.

We can also connect with energies available from a wide range of sources including minerals, crystals, plants, trees, elementals, fairies, angels, earth spirit i.e. Lady Gaia and the green man, and source, God and all that is. And this list is far from exhaustive.

Some of the energy we carry with us is fear-based i.e. there is not enough to go around and I have to compete with you for the limited resources that we have.

Much of the energy we carry with us is love. There is plenty to go around and I honour the process of receiving and giving for we are separate and we are one.

The third point to balance what otherwise emerges as a polarity is fully-informed choice. Being able to see both sides and make a choice based on freewill.

Because we are in the process of consciously choosing to be ourselves it may be as well to cleanse and protect our spiritual space and vibration.

There follows a simple routine for doing this. This can start each day, it may be the start of meditation, or on any occasion when it is important to clear the energy around you.

This is a routine where energies of pure unconditional love are requested which dissolve and transmute thoughts which have aggregated in fear which are dense and clogging.

Find a quiet space and time.

Close your eyes and bring your awareness back to yourself with one or two breaths.

Now imagine a candle flame in front of you. On the outside it is composed of three primary colours. These are gold, silver and violet.

Ask that the flame get larger until it is life-size and see yourself stepping into it.

In your mind's eye the flame envelopes you. Feel or sense it cleansing and stay in this life-size flame for one or two minutes. It's possible you will start to feel lighter and maybe notice the change in the air around you which can become lighter and sweeter.

Once you feel that energies around you have changed ask that your life-size flame divide into three parts.

The first part you send from the soles of your feet down into the ground to blaze and clear a connection which you are making with the energy at the core of the earth. The flame will burn ahead and clear your connection with the earth's core.

You are connecting with energy which creates matter. You may know this energy as Lady Gaia or mother earth, and Sanat Kumara, or the green man. These energies are masculine and feminine and they are joining to create a new balanced energy.

To carry forward the discussion in this book the energy has been named Saul.

Now bring your attention to the top third of your flame.

Ask that this third of the flame move from the crown of your head along the connection you have to your higher self, and from your higher self to your guardian angel, your spirit guides, and to source, the creator and all that is.

You are connecting to a new light and a source of energy which is being returned to the earth after a long absence. It is a balance of male and female energies. You may sense these as Jesus Christ and Mary Magdalene, or as Krishna and Radha, or Yin and Yang.

The joining together of male and female has made one which is also a third and this new energy has been called Sarah in this book.

Now bring your attention to the middle and remaining part of the flame. Ask or direct that this flame move within your body to cleanse, clear and stimulate your energy system or chakra system.

Your energy system is made up of many energy points some of which are regarded as major points some minor. These energy points are also called chakras and the words are interchangeable. The classic 7 energy or chakra points are used here although this sequence of using the gold, silver and violet flame will cleanse and develop all of your chakras.

See in your minds eye the flame moving from the soles of your feet, which take you on your journey, via the energy points at your knees which provide movement and the ability to hold still, up to your root chakra at the base of your spine. The root is the first of the 7 major classic chakras.

The root energy point provides much of our grounding as spiritual beings in human form and it is in this place in our energy system that we know when we feel safe and secure.

Let the flame stay here whilst it cleanses and gently starts to open your chakra. The colour of this chakra is usually a deep red and the flame will burn off any shadows or flecks of other colours.

It is also important to pay attention to the connection between your chakras, i.e. the thread or column which connects your energy system along which the flame moves and along which the new energy will move.

From your root chakra move the flame along to your sacral, which is the width of two fingers below your tummy button. The sacral is the energy of sociability, community, and also stores the energy for much of our creativity including our sexual and sensual nature. The colour of this chakra is usually orange.

Again take time for the flame to cleanse and rejuvenate the energy point. At any of the chakras the flame may move through quickly or may stay awhile to cleanse and clear. Simply allow the process to achieve what it needs for you.

From your sacral move the flame along to the solar plexus which is just below the ribcage and at the top of your tummy. In the solar plexus we hold many of our emotions including emotions which we have denied or otherwise repressed. The colour of this chakra is usually yellow or gold. The solar plexus is also where we find or determine our courage and integrity.

Allow the flame to cleanse and clear the passage or route from the sacral to the solar plexus and allow time at the solar plexus to cleanse and for the flame to gently rotate or move the energy.

Sometimes the connection between the solar plexus and the heart can become blocked so be aware of the progress of your flame and of where it needs to stop and take longer to refresh your system.

The heart is love. It is our connection to source, creator and the love that is all there is. The heart knows love to be infinite but our experience as humans is to regulate this love.

Whilst the flame is cleansing your heart consider if you wish to adjust the regulation of the flow. Perhaps to receive a little more and to give a little more love. The colour of the heart is usually pink on the outside and green at the centre.

From your heart the flame will move along to the energy point in your throat. This is where we speak our truth and express our identity. The colour of the throat chakra is usually blue which can range from a mild or soft blue through to an intense cobalt blue.

There is sometimes a turquoise blue between the heart and the throat which appears to be a combination of the heart green and the throat blue and signifies a connection or expression of universal love.

Allow the flame to cleanse and clear your system and to gently rotate or move the throat chakra so that energy may flow.

The next energy point is your third eye through which we develop our senses of the psyche i.e. unseen energies and the spiritual. The colour of this chakra is usually indigo or a deep navy blue. The third eye can appear also in a variety of shapes perhaps as a diamond shape with many facets or simply as an eye.

Finally the crown chakra is usually pure or pearlescent white and purple. The crown regulates the flow of spiritual energy from source, the creator, all that is.

Once you have cleansed your energy system bring all three parts of the flame together and reduce the size of the flame. Now send the reduced size flame gently, along the entire system and form the intention that this will also draw the energies of the earth and energies from source and all that is through your system but very gently at first.

This is like doing a conga dance

To do this. Send the reduced size flame down to the earth's core. Ask to gently draw the new balanced energy of Saul, along your earth connection, up through the soles of your feet, through your chakra or energy system and out through the crown of your head. The flame is leading the way and the new energy is linking along behind.

You take the flame with the linked earth energy up to your higher self, your spiritual guides and to source, the creator and all that is.

You return the flame, this time leading a new balanced male and female energy from spirit called Sarah, back down your spiritual connection or thread, and through your crown and gently down through your energy system, through the soles of your feet and all the way down to the earth's core.

Once you feel cleansed, energized and refreshed by these energies you can bring the flow of these energies into your heart. These are Saul, from the earth's core up as far as your heart chakra, and Sarah, from source, down as far as your heart. There the two balanced energies can join to create one and a third, a new energy called Gandana. Let this energy gently flow from your heart into your aura i.e. the energy field around you.

If you wish you can direct this energy elsewhere, for instance to someone you know who needs healing, maybe to a situation or relationship which would benefit from love and balance.

To close down or reduce the flow of this energy thank the source of these energies and ask that the flow slows to a point where it is barely perceptible. Then gently reduce the flow of energy through your energy system by asking your chakras to reduce the flow. Say on a dial or measure from 5 out of 10 to 1 out of 10.

Opening your heart

Our truth is internal. We know that love in our heart is infinite and inexhaustible. The amount of love we receive and the amount that we give we regulate. Some of 'the rules' about the flow will depend upon our acceptance or rejection of honouring life and honouring others. And much of that will depend in turn upon our life experiences.

A quote I am reminded of at this point comes from Marianne Williamson who wrote in "A return to love":

'At a certain point we forgive because we decide to forgive. Healing occurs in the present, not the past. We are not held back by the love we did not receive in the past, but by the love we're not extending in the present.'[11]

Change is always in the present moment.

If the idea of checking out how your heart is doing at the present moment appeals to you the following exercise might help.

Find a quiet space and time where there will be no disturbances.

Close your eyes and bring your awareness into your own space and become aware of your body.

Form the intention that you will be making a journey into your body. Decide on your mode of transport. This can be anything you want, a camel ride, canoe, fly a plane, ride a bike, do the journey on a pogo stick etc.

Equip your self for the journey. You'll need a torch or powerful light of some description. Maybe a travelling companion. A

---

[11] From "A Return to Love" by Marianne Williamson. Thorsons. 1996 revised edition. P.175

spirit guide maybe, or your guardian angel, or your nan. It needs to be someone who you know loves you without question and who will give you advice for your highest good.

When you are ready start your journey and let your first stop be at your heart chakra. Here you gently enter your body and have a good look around. Switch on your light. Make your way to your heart.

What do you see? What does the landscape look like, what does the heart muscle look like, do you have barriers up in front of your heart or other forms of defence and fortification?

Have a good look around and see if the landscape reflects how you are feeling about yourself in your current life. Is it an accurate reflection or are there adjustments you would like to make?

If you wish to have a consultation with your travel companion(s) at any time do so. Possibly they can bring another perspective.

Make any adjustments or changes you think are necessary. Maybe drop some of the armour? Whatever changes you make be sure that you feel comfortable with them.

Check around outside your heart too to ensure the area is tidy and things are healthy. If things here need to change make the changes.

Now decide that you are entering your heart. Find the entrance, a doorway, and go inside. Find yourself in the reception chamber. Check how this is. What are you feeling? What are you seeing?

From the reception room there is an adjoining chamber where you can meet directly with your soul. Everything about you is known or can be accessed from here and you can experience and know yourself as pure love in this chamber.

When you are ready go inside. Ask any questions you may have, work out any issues, all of the answers are here. This is your time, your space, your life.

When you are ready prepare to leave. Make any adjustments you wish as you go. Return the way you came. Collect your travel companions and take your vehicle or mode of transport to bring you back through your heart chakra.

Now bring your awareness gently but firmly back into your whole physical body. Be aware of your physical body sitting on a seat with your feet on the floor, or lying down and the weight of your body on the bed. Wriggle your toes and fingers, and in your own time gently open your eyes and come back fully into the room.

Once you are sure of the lay-out of your heart and that you can open your heart and make communication, accessing your heart can be done in three breaths.

Find a quiet space and time. Close your eyes.

Take a breath to centre or ground yourself and let go of day-to-day thoughts.

On the next breath feel the breath in your lungs and say, I am that I am.

On your third breath feel the breath enter your heart and take your awareness with the breath and talk, listen or be with your heart.

Continue to breath normally and come back when you are ready.

Merge with the grail energies

The grail energy is formed by the concept of three points, a trinity. The eternal triangle is of peace, harmony and unconditional love. The earth triangle which matches the eternal triangle is of receiving, giving and honouring. These triangles may form a bridge, meet and merge to form a six-pointed star.

The grail trinity also helps to draw in masculine and feminine energies which are creating new life and new energy. Masculine and feminine join to become one and create a third which is the process of creation.

And it is the same for us. Each of us living a life, here, now, are a combination of a spiritual being and a human being.

On earth we were born of masculine and feminine energy. Our mother and father. The two become one to create a third. You.

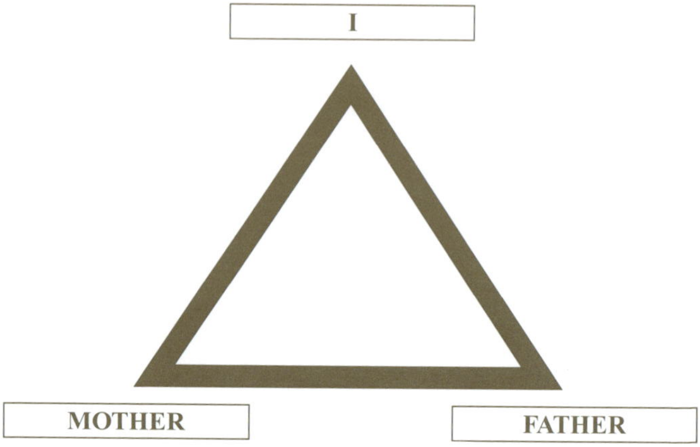

We are also spiritual beings and therefore have a matching triangle in spirit. Mother, father, and you.

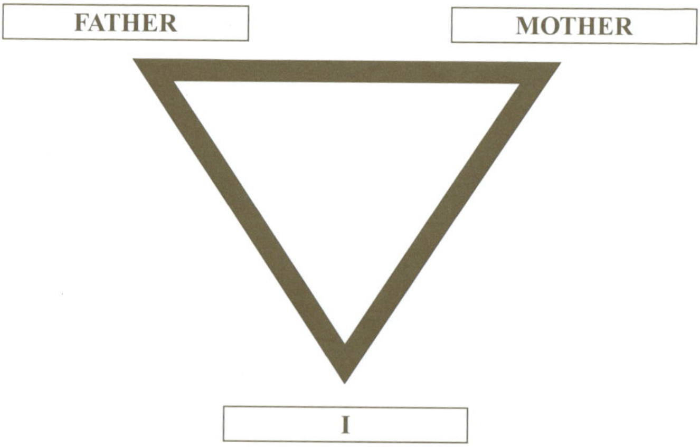

In similar ways in which we experimented with grail energies take your time to see how you feel about the energies which you represent and which you bring with you.

For instance you can ask your spirit triangle and your earth triangle to form a bridge and make communication

Close your eyes and tune into this energy that is you. How does this feel?

You are here as a spiritual being in human form. Look for the frisson, the inner knowing, the spark that will bring to you your inner truth. Besides being a portal for matter and spirit to meet, do you bring in grail energy?

The triangles which represent you can meet. This is the point which many who have studied and practiced a spiritual path call self-realisation. A knowing and realisation of ourself as being human and spiritual at the same time.

Our knowledge of the grail however, says that these two parts can join to become one which is a third. A new being who has masculine and feminine energy. Who is human and who is spirit. Who knows the ways of the earth and knows the ways of spirit. And this is the process of things becoming actual. Realising and being ourself.

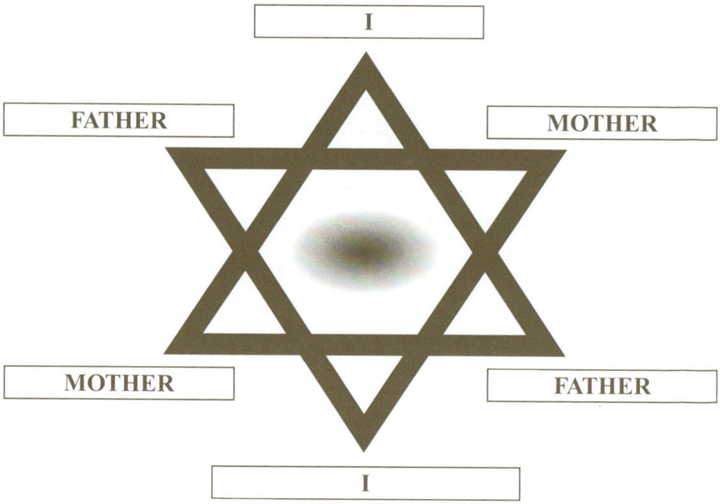

This in essence is a building block of creation. The joining of spirit and matter to create one and a third. Mathematically this may be expressed as Pi.

It brings with it a fresh perspective on co-creation, or co-creating with source, the creator and all that is, as well as support for your inner knowing that you are a child of the universe.

Take your time with experiencing these energies and with asking questions. As always the answers you are looking for are within.

If you find that yourself as energy from the earth and yourself as energy from spirit were not ready to meet or merge don't worry. It's likely in that case that you are not ready at this time for this to happen and it will happen later.

As with all things check yourself out. I'm reminded of what they might say in Ireland. You might be asked 'How are you?' and you'll say 'fine thanks' and they'll say with a bit of Mrs Doyle-like persistence 'no really, how are you within yourself?'

How to bring the awareness of yourself, and awareness of the new light and new energy for the purpose of co-creating is the subject of the next chapter.

Go Direct

The realisation and making actual in our own experience that we are created both in human and spiritual form to be a new creative energy in our world brings along new perspectives to our life.

We can actively create the life we choose. We can release fears, bring in love, let the sun shine on our lives in vast, numerous and wonderful ways.

As creative spiritual beings we can work with source, the creator and all that is to direct how we wish to live life.

This has been understood and acted upon by people who are working and creating the life they choose. Some of these people have learned these and related perspectives via the system of healing which has been developed and taught by Vianna Stibal and her organization 'nature's path' since Viana cured herself of cancer in 1996. The healing is called theta-healing.[12]

As a child of the universe you may direct your life as you choose.

If you wish to experience this find a quiet space and time.

In your minds eye see yourself as an earth triangle and yourself as a spirit triangle. Let these form and communicate with each other. Check to see where these triangles are in relation to each other and direct that they merge.

If you find that your own energies as human and spirit are not ready to meet and merge at this time bring in the grail star by forming an earth triangle, and ask for the eternal triangle from

---

[12] I am not describing theta healing which is a complete and discreet system of healing in its own right. For more information about theta look-up www.thetahealing.com

source to meet and merge with it. How this is done is outlined in part two of this book under the chapter 'is this the holy grail?'

Allow your own experience to determine what you do and honour your intuition above all else.

Once your triangles have formed and have merged bring the star you have formed into your heart. The grail star brings with it the energy of peace, harmony and unconditional love, merged with receiving, giving and honouring all life.

Now bring in a gold, silver and violet flame. Let the flame grow until it is life-size and when it feels comfortable step into it.

Let this flame cleanse your energy or auric field and let it cleanse within you.

Now see in the centre of your flame the pure white light. Pearlescent. It lights up the six-pointed star in your heart. Move into the centre of this flame and into the centre of your grail star to meet with source, creator, and all that is.

In this energy your life is created and can be actively directed by you in accordance with your highest good and in balance with all that is.

It can help enormously to seek clarity of intention and the route to clarity is usually to begin with a process of release and forgiveness.

Release is usually of fear or fear which has grown with self-belief which has now outlived its purpose. Be discerning about what you need and what is no longer useful. For instance a belief that you may get burnt if you touch a hot stove or may get knocked down by an on-coming car if you stand in the road is useful. A belief that you are responsible for original sin may not be useful to you.

Find a form of words with which you are comfortable, which reflect the principle that you are a spiritual being within a human body, and that you are co-creating your life with the energies which brought you life and this experience.

For example "Working with the energies of creation I now direct that I release all fear-based criticism of myself"

Work out how you will know that this has happened. In theta–healing this is called witnessing. Within your inner-flame space and with your eyes closed take up a position outside yourself and witness the removal of this belief.

Let it take the form that it represents for you. Ask that whatever is released or removed be replaced by the unconditional love of source and creator of all that is.

And finally acknowledge the removal and bring yourself back into your body. A form of words like "Thankyou. It is done. So be it" and consciously move from your position as an observer outside the body back inside to your heart.

You can test yourself for beliefs which you hold and which you may have no conscious awareness of holding by forms of muscle-testing which have been developed through the study of Kinesiology.

The simplest of these is to find north. Stand up and face yourself in that direction. Work out which movement represents a 'yes' answer for you and which movement represents 'no'. So close your eyes and say 'yes' and see how your body moves. Close your eyes and say 'no' and see which way your body moves. This is your way of knowing positive and negative.

You can also use this simple form of divination for other questions about yourself. For instance, is bread healthy for me to eat ? along with many other uses.

It is possible that you will find you are carrying beliefs which come as quite a surprise to you so follow your intuition and hunches or work with others who you trust and who you sense can help to release beliefs which have outlived their purpose.[13]

In any event try out some beliefs which have been with us for quite a time and see if you have picked these up from a previous life or via information and awareness which has filtered down to you from your ancestors. For instance test whether you believe

'I am responsible for original sin' or

'I believe that men are better than women' or

'All strangers are dangerous'

or maybe 'When I die I will cease to exist'

If these and other beliefs test yes for you *and you wish to change them* go back to your form of words and direct that they are released, witness the release, ask for the release to be replaced with the unconditional love of source, say thankyou and acknowledge the change. And bring yourself consciously back into your body.

Forgiveness follows a similar pattern. It allows love to be

---

[13] For instance in the group I studied with we were taken by surprise when the group facilitator, Valeria Moore, said she kept seeing blue-feet. Between us we pieced together a tribe or alliance of Picts and Celts who vigorously opposed the Roman occupation of England. Identity was formed by dying the feet and legs of those in the tribal alliance blue, and a formidable and detailed fear-based oath and blood tie of fealty to the 'tribe' was registered by all of us which we were still holding onto within our belief system.

received and love to be given, and for life to take on a new dimension where it is possible to honour the light and life in all things.

Decide who you wish to forgive. If this is painful initially you can do this in stages by directing that light be shed on the situation so that you can see past your pain to the experience which you sought to receive.

When you are ready to forgive move into the pearlescent white space in the middle of your grail star and in the middle of the gold, silver and violet flame and direct that it is done.

It may be important to forgive yourself too. Find a form of words which feels accurate. For instance

'Working with the energies of creation I direct that I forgive X for the pain I have held and I forgive myself too knowing that I was doing the best that I knew how to at the time'.

Witness the forgiveness and the removal of the pain from your body and say thankyou.

Bring yourself firmly back into your body.

Being a co-creator you may also direct that others release fears, illness, physical and mental impairments and much more besides providing that you have the permission of the other person.[14]

---

[14] If this form of healing appeals to you then look into theta healing which offers a complete training structure

Living from the heart

Working consciously with your heart means taking care that it is nourished and exercised. As you might expect this entails balance in what you eat and drink, taking regular physical exercise, and getting good quality sleep.

Drink plenty of fresh, clean water, and take to heart the information that is available to us from the photography of water crystals by Dr Masaru Emoto.[15] Ask that your water be blessed.

Two further exercises might be helpful to a life where we live from the heart. The first is to return to the chapter entitled 'breathe' in section one of this book and ensure that you breathe for 12 breaths each day in equal thirds into your stomach, lungs and heart, and shoulders and throat. Combining the breath with affirmations such as those outlined in that chapter can help provide a depth of experience.

The other exercise is to consciously bring grail energy and light into your heart.

For this you'll need a quiet space and time. Sit or lie comfortably. Close your eyes.

In your mind's eye form your flame of gold, silver and violet. Let it be life-sized and see yourself walk into it. Allow the flames to cleanse and lighten the energy around you and within you.

Now find the white, pearlescent centre of the flame and enter that. Within the white, still centre of the flame begin to construct the grail star. The grail star is made of an eternal triangle of

---

[15] There are a number of examples of water crystals which have been treated in different ways on the web at www.whatthebleep.com/crystals . Some have been blessed. Some have been discouraged or have been shouted at with abusive language, some have been through a microwave. Just when you thought it was safe to go into the kitchen!

peace, harmony and unconditional love which merges with an earth triangle of receiving, giving and honouring life.

Once these triangles have merged allow white and gold light to pour from the grail star directly into your heart. Be gentle with this exercise until you are familiar with the grail energy and with opening your heart.

The point of the exercise is to nourish and stimulate your heart, the centre where you are connected to universal love, separate and one as a new creative being. The love that is available to you and that you express is infinite.

Take your time and allow your heart to come along at its own pace.

To close the exercise allow the grail star to enter your heart if that feels comfortable. Step back from the white centre of the flame and see the gold, silver and violet flame around you.

Now step back from this flame and bring yourself gently but firmly into your physical body.

Wriggle your fingers and toes and when you are ready open your eyes and come back into the room.

Drink plenty of fresh, clean and blessed water.

Conclusion

In many respects we have come full circle and are back where we started. It's your life, your choice. This full circle can take the shape of a spiral which allows the energy to turn and evolve.

Along the way there have been exercises designed to reconnect with life and the wonder of being alive.

There has also been the finding of the grail and uncovering some of the principles which have kept it hidden from view.

The grail as presented in this book arrives in a 'V' shape. This signifies balance and the realization of trinity on earth. The 'V' also represents the birth of new energy which is balanced and which is created in all of us.

Everything about the grail points to it being an experience. Within the grail energies amazing things happen. When enough of us have experience of the grail energies there is a sense of the energy forming a new way of being and delivering a new light. This could be the birth of a new civilisation.

In concluding it is a privilege to say I honour the light and life within you. The light we are carrying is separate and it is the same. It is more brilliant, more marvellous, more wonderful than I imagined.

Thankyou

Namasté

Also by Declan Kerr

"How to heal with angels"

Starting with introductory questions like what is good health, who are angels and why heal with them? the guide takes the reader through a step-by-step description of how to heal with angels in a clear and accessible style

There is discussion and description of healing for ourselves and healing for others as well as consideration of specific conditions including IBS and eating disorders

Also by aaah publications

"Finding your inner peace" by Ladan Ratcliffe

The cards present each of the 12 major chakras or energy points in the body in different stages of flow. Each card illustration carries a unique vibration with interpretations of the cards and key words alongside the illustrations and in a handy booklet.

There are 48 cards in total, four for each chakra and 4 for insight and understanding about the chakra system overall.

The cards introduce a magical energy in holistic self-healing and inspire spiritual development